Just What the Doctor Ordered

Just What the Doctor Ordered

The History of American Medicine

Brandon Marie Miller

 Lerner Publications Company • Minneapolis

For Elinore Luke Schlenker,
a.k.a. Peggy. Thanks, Mom!

My appreciation to editor Margaret Goldstein for her skillful
manuscript surgery. Thanks also to Joseph McAuliffe for generously
sharing his knowledge of pharmacopeia.

Copyright © 1997 by Brandon Marie Miller

Library of Congress Cataloging-in-Publication Data

Miller, Brandon Marie.
   Just what the doctor ordered : the history of American medicine / Brandon
Marie Miller.
      p.   cm.
   Includes bibliographical references and index.
   Summary: Traces the history of medicine in North America, from the
remedies used by native peoples to the medical advances and health trends of
the twentieth century.
   ISBN 0-8225-1737-X (alk. paper)
   1. Medicine—North America—History—Juvenile literature. [1. Medicine—
History] I. Title.
R150.M53   1997
610'.973—dc20   95-51491

Manufactured in the United States of America
1 2 3 4 5 6 - JR - 02 01 00 99 98 97

Contents

"THE MYSTERY AND POWER OF THINGS"

For my own part, I would prefer an old Indian before any chirurgeon [surgeon] . . . both for the certainty, ease, and speediness of cure.

　　　—James Adair, white trader among
　　　　　　　the Cherokee, 1775

For five months in the winter of 1535–36, three ships commanded by French explorer Jacques Cartier lay trapped in the frozen waters of the Saint Lawrence River. After weeks with only shipboard supplies to eat, many of the 110-man crew fell ill. Body aches and weariness soon gave way to swollen gums, blackened teeth, stinking breath, and swollen legs covered in black bruises. Twenty-five men died, and many others lay near death.

"Then it pleased God," noted Cartier in his journal, "to sent us the knowledge of remedie of our healthes and recoverie." The Frenchmen watched a band of Indians trudging along the snowy riverbank. An older Indian man seemed to suffer from the same disease gripping the sailors. But several days later, when the Indians passed again, the sick man walked along looking perfectly healthy and cured.

Cartier climbed down onto the ice and approached the native people. He explained that illness had struck his men, but didn't reveal how vulnerable the disease had left the crew. The cured man, who was the band's chief, sent several women into the woods to gather a certain tree bark. By boiling bark and water into a thick syrup, the Indian women prepared a medicine.

At first the sickly Frenchmen feared drinking the strange brew concocted by "wild savages." But what choice did they have except death? A few days later, the sailors felt better, amazed by the Indians' medical skills. As one man reported, all the French drugs could "not have done so much in one yere, as that tree did in six days."

Over thousands of years, Native Americans had developed many useful medicines and treatments. In the case of this disease—called scurvy—the Indians did not know the cause. Their knowledge of a successful remedy, however, surpassed the learning of Europe. The tree bark boiled and served to Cartier's men in 1536 probably contained vitamin C, identified centuries later as a preventative and a cure for scurvy.

"I CRIED TO THE SPIRIT OF THE WORLD"

Native Americans of many tribes viewed good health as a balance between body, mind, and spirit. Certain conditions could destroy that balance. Indians believed people might grow sick if they violated a tribal taboo. Perhaps a hunter had not said the right prayer before making a kill. Had the patient eaten a forbidden food? Had a holy ritual been forgotten? Evil forces might also cause disease. Witches were thought to send illness through the dark of night. A thieving spirit could steal a patient's soul.

Curing sickness and restoring the body's balance required special remedies, given by medicine men (and sometimes medicine women). Medicine men, or shamans, possessed a deep understanding of the spirit world. Respected members of the tribe, they performed many roles, acting as healers, seers into the future, teachers, priests, and sorcerers. Sometimes they were feared for the powers at their command. An Oglala Lakota medicine man named Black Elk described his role as a healer:

Of course it was not I who cured. It was the power from the outer world, and the visions and ceremonies had only made me like a hole through which the power could come to the two-leggeds [humans]. If I thought I was doing it myself, the hole would close up and no power could come through.

Indians passed on the secrets of their doctoring skills from one generation to the next. Elder medicine men trained younger ones in ceremonies and songs, chants and prayers, and the preparation of medicines. Women often served as herbalists—experts in preparing medicines from herbs and plants. A Comanche woman could not learn medicine unless she had a medicine man husband. If he died, she was free to treat patients on her own.

Initiation ceremony for an Ojibwa medicine man

In some tribes, special medicine societies trained healers. To join the Ojibwa Midewiwin Medicine Society, a man had to study for seven years. Members of the Iroquois False Face Society wore carved wooden masks—sometimes inspired by a vision—to cure sickness. In spring and fall, society members danced in masks and ragged clothing, shaking rattles, before going house to house banishing evil and sickness from the village. The Arikara tribe had nine orders of medicine men, each order governed by an animal spirit. To capture the animal's mystical powers, healers wore costumes made from its fur or feathers.

Medicine men carried special tools for healing the sick. A medicine bundle made of animal skin held herbs, roots, sacred plant pollens, and charms to ward off evil. The bundle might be handed down through a family. In some tribes, every male—and often many females—carried a medicine bundle.

George B. Grinnell, chronicler of the northern Cheyenne, explained:

> All these things which we speak of as medicine the Indians call mysterious, and when he calls them mysterious this only means that they are beyond his power to account for. . . . He whom we call a medicine man may be a doctor, a healer of diseases; or if he is a worker of magic, he is a mystery man.

CURES AND TREATMENTS

The rumble of drums carried an offering to the Great Spirit. The shaking of rattles and the low chant of prayers filled the dwelling. With a rattlesnake fang, the medicine man opened a small slit in the patient's skin. Then, using a hollow bit of bone, stick, or horn, he sucked an evil object from the patient's body—an object perhaps only hidden in his own clothes and pulled out to show the patient.

The "sucking cure" was not just a sham to relieve the patient's mind. It had a valid medical effect. Through this practice, the medicine man sucked up and spit out poison from snakebites, as well as pus gathering in wounds. In the mid-1700s, a white observer noted how the Choctaw tribe treated a bullet wound:

> The medicine man first sucks the wound then spits out the blood . . . they blow into it a powder made of root. Another root powder is used to dry and heal the wound, and still other roots are used in a solution with which the wound is bathed to help prevent gangrene.

Indians of almost every tribe purified body and mind and drove out disease by taking sweat baths in special huts. By pouring water seasoned with herbs over hot rocks, bathers filled the hut with thick clouds of cleansing steam. Afterward, bathers might plunge into a river, have a massage, or rest. One Englishman marveled that the Indians "take great delight in Sweating, and therefore in every Town they have a Sweating-House, and a Doctor is paid by the Publick to attend it."

For the most part, Native Americans practiced better hygiene than their white neighbors. As one white physician wrote in 1850, Indian "men, women, and children, from early infancy, are in the daily habit of bathing during the warm months and not infrequently after cold weather has set in." The same doctor, noting that bathing preserved good health, observed, "our [white] population seldom bathe at all . . . it is much to be regretted, that the practice cannot be made more general."

Native Americans learned much about how the body worked by observing animals. They knew that the lungs breathed, the heart pumped blood, and the brain was the organ of thought. While some tribes drew small amounts of "bad blood" to treat illness, the practice of bleeding was not widespread. As one early settler learned from the Algonquin Indians:

> The Blood being the Taper of Life, we have more occasion to pour it in than to take it out . . . after loss of Blood nature acts feebly and heavily, the Intrails are over-heated, and the Parts are dry'd, which gives rise to all the Diseases that afflict the Europeans.

Indian people set broken bones with cloth and wooden splints. The Pimas made splints from the ribs of giant cactus. For cleansing wounds, Potawatomis and Ojibwas created simple syringes out of animal bladders and quills. Wounds were stitched with human hair and vegetable fibers, then cleansed with boiled water and herbs. A white man reported in 1788 on the Ojibwa technique for repairing torn earlobes: "They cut them smooth with a knife, and sew the parts together with a needle and deer's sinews, and after sweating in a stove, resume their usual cheerfulness."

Animal fats and fish oils were slathered on the skin for massage, as insect repellents, and as buffers against the cold. Favorite treatments for rheumatism were steam baths, soaking in natural hot springs, and massages. "When sick they only drink Broth and eat sparingly," wrote a European about the Algonquin. The Iroquois treated fever with rest, sweating, and a liquid diet.

Whites, who suffered much from tooth decay, noted that Native Americans had fewer problems with their teeth. Indian diets rarely included sticky sweets. Cavities were plugged with herbs, tobacco leaves, or purple coneflowers. Some tribes chewed prickly ash bark for toothaches or rinsed their mouths with tea brewed from dogwood.

Sometimes the pain became too great, and a diseased tooth needed pulling. One tribe used a hammer and chisel technique. The doctor dislodged the bad tooth by striking it with a leather cane—a process that caused "half the pain" white dentistry would have inflicted, claimed a white observer.

"I MADE A PRAYER TO THE HERB"

One white missionary noted that Indian medicine consisted of "various roots and plants known to themselves, the properties of which they are not fond of disclosing to strangers. They make considerable use of the barks of trees." Sassafras, dogwood, spruce, birch, and other trees served as medicine chests. Bark was boiled into teas, pounded into powders and pulpy poultices, and chewed. Leaves, resins, and roots also provided medicines. A root called ipecacuanha, or ipecac, induced vomiting.

In 1884 white physicians learned the benefit of cocaine for killing pain. Native Americans had known the value of the coca plant's leaves for hundreds of years. Another Native American painkiller was jimsonweed.

Willow bark contained a natural ingredient similar to aspirin. Rotten grains of corn, dried and pounded, helped heal sores. Oak bark was a natural antiseptic, used to cleanse wounds. Smoke from cedar twigs relieved head colds. Boiled with berries, prickly ash bark made a cough syrup. A French priest, Father Gabriel Sagard, observed that Huron medicine men "always carry with them a bag full of herbs and drugs, to doctor the sick."

THE WHITE MAN'S VIEW

During the 1600s, newly arrived Europeans generally frowned upon Indian medicine, so closely tied to tribal religion. White missionaries feared that Indian medicine masked the devil's work. Father Sagard noticed that a Huron medicine man isolated (quarantined) sick people from the rest of the village "so that he may practice upon him there during the night his devilish contrivances." Yet the priest recognized that the practice helped prevent others from getting ill. "This is a most excellent custom . . . " he conceded, "which indeed ought to be adopted in every country."

Dr. Edwin Jones, who explored the Rocky Mountain region in 1819 and 1820, declared the Omaha tribe's medical knowledge "very inconsiderable" and based only on superstitions and ceremonies. But some white doctors recognized the benefits of Native American practices, such as the use of massage for delivering babies and the afterbirth. "Although constantly practiced by primitive people for thousands of years," read one study, "these methods have been recently rediscovered by learned men . . . and given to the world as new."

Europeans also commented on the good health of native people, crediting "the harmony that prevails among them. They have no law-suits and take little pains to acquire the goods of this life, for which we Christians torment ourselves so much." One Englishman described Indians as "strong and sound of body, well fed, without blemish." "There are not so many Diseases raigning amongst them as our Europeans," commented another colonist from England. Almost two centuries later, Stephen Long

Indian healers wore animal skins to capture an animal's special powers.

reported from his western expedition of 1819 and 1820: "[The Indians] catalogue of diseases, and morbid affections, is infinitely less extensive than that of civilized men."

But a life spent outdoors did affect Native American health. Digestive complaints were common. The elderly suffered from arthritis and pneumonia. Sunlight and smoky fires harmed eyesight. Rare, however, were cancer, heart diseases, and illnesses caused by diet deficiencies. Tragically, the overall good health enjoyed by Native Americans did not survive after whites arrived on the scene.

"DISEASES WE HAVE NO NAME FOR"

Not warfare but diseases—diseases unknown to Native Americans before the arrival of Europeans—wiped out huge numbers of Indian people. Smallpox, diphtheria, typhoid, cholera, measles, and tuberculosis struck blow after blow. Perhaps almost 90 percent of the Indians on the

Two of only 31 Mandans who survived a 1837 smallpox epidemic

East Coast died of disease during the 1600s—the first century white colonists arrived to stay.

Indian medicines—and white medicines of the same period—were ineffective against these diseases. But whites, from centuries of exposure, had built up some natural immunity to the infections. Native Americans had no protection.

Smallpox ravaged the tribes of New England. Whole villages, hundreds of people, died. By 1780, only one-fourth of the Cherokee nation had survived attacks of smallpox. Tuberculosis destroyed the Onondaga in New York State. The terrible story was repeated as white settlers moved west. Only 31 Mandans—from a tribe of 1,600—survived an 1837 onslaught of smallpox. Naturalist John James Audubon reported from the West in 1842: "It is said that in the various attacks of this scourge [smallpox], 52,000 Indians have perished." In 1849, 200 Cheyenne families died from cholera. Measles epidemics struck the Indians of the Northwest and the Lakotas several times during the 1800s.

Yet Native American medicine survived. Often, white settlers on the frontier—and white physicians—turned to the remedies Indians had developed over centuries of practice.

"DEATH COMES GALLOPING"

*The nature of the country is such
that it causes much sicknes.*
                    —Richard Frethorne,
            Jamestown, Virginia, 1623

O n the morning of May 13, 1607, three English ships anchored off
a finger of land jutting into Virginia's James River. Here, 105 eager but
unprepared settlers built the first permanent English settlement in the
New World. They called it Jamestown, in honor of King James I. At first
the site seemed to offer advantages, but problems soon outweighed the
benefits. Swarms of disease-carrying mosquitoes infested the colonists'
new marshy home—a home that lacked even fresh drinking water.
Jamestown, birthplace of a new nation, began amid sickness and death.

"Our men," wrote George Percy, "were destroyed with cruell diseases
as Swellings, Flixes, Burning Fevers . . . but for the most part they died
of meere famine. There was never Englishmen left in a forreigne Coun-
trey in such miserie as wee were in this new discovered Virginia." Even
with aid from the Native Americans around Jamestown, half of the

colonists died before September. When a ship arrived in January 1608, loaded with new supplies and men, only 38 original settlers were left to greet them.

Worse days lay ahead. By autumn of 1609, new recruits from England swelled Jamestown's population to around 500. But that winter, typhoid and dysentery swept through the village. Food ran out; a few people resorted to eating the dead. "That time . . . we called the starving time," wrote one who survived, "it was too vile to say, and scarce to be beleeved, what we endured." By spring, a mere 60 settlers still lived.

Under new leadership, Jamestown hung on. When fear of Indian attack trapped the population inside the fort, settlers drew up rules "to cleanse the Town." Tossing used water into the street and washing clothes within 20 feet of the drinking well were forbidden. So the fort would not be "choaked and poisoned with ill aires," anyone who dared "do the necessities of nature" within a quarter mile of the stockade was punished. Colonists were ordered to keep their houses "sweete and cleane."

With disease hanging over the colony's shoulder, Jamestown grew very slowly. From 1607 to 1625, about 6,500 people immigrated to Virginia. Yet a census record from 1625 shows a population of only 1,025. After years of hardship, Indian wars, and infighting among the colonists, Jamestown was abandoned around 1699 for a new capital at Williamsburg.

North of Virginia, on the weather-beaten coast of Massachusetts, a second English settlement clung to life in the New World. In 1620, the pilgrims at "Plimoth Plantation" faced many of the same hardships as the Jamestown colonists. William Bradford, an early governor of the colony, described the pilgrims' first winter:

> But that which was most sadd . . . was, that in 2 or 3 moneths time halfe of their company dyed, espetialy in Jan: and February, being the depth of winter, and wanting houses and other comforts; being infected with the scurvie and other diseases, which this long vioage . . . had brought upon them . . . that of 100 and odd persons, scarce 50 remained. And of these in the time of most distres, ther was but 6 or 7 sound persons.

This colony survived with the help of Native Americans and—as with Jamestown—the arrival of fresh settlers.

Where were the doctors to treat so many sick? Few trained physicians or "chirurgeons" left the comfort of England for the wilds of America. The London Company and the Massachusetts Bay Company (the groups overseeing colonial settlement) hired physicians for one- and two-year terms to serve in the colonies. But often, these were not the best doctors that money could buy. Most medical care rested in the hands of poorly trained and uneducated people.

With the absence of trained doctors in America, others took on the job. Women served as healers, both to their own families and as midwives for other women during childbirth. Clergymen, the most educated and respected members of a town, dispensed advice on bodily ills as well as troubled souls. Most colonial Americans agreed with the words one doctor wrote in his ledger: "Sin is the Cause of all Diseases, and sometimes Diseases are immediately sent by God, and he alone must take them away by himself."

PHYSICIANS AND OTHER PEOPLE

A young colonist who wished to learn medicine studied with a doctor—if one was available. Apprenticeships lasted from five to seven years. During that time, the student could not marry, gamble, or frequent taverns or theaters. Complete obedience was expected. An apprentice cared for the doctor's horse, swept the office, collected fees, and delivered medicines. By studying the doctor's collection of medical books and observing treatments, the apprentice learned enough about medicine to call himself a doctor too—even though the books were often out of date and the treatments ineffective. Several African slaves learned medicine from their doctor-masters and eventually gained their freedom and the right to practice on their own.

In Europe, the title "physician" referred to someone with a university medical education. Surgeons and apothecaries (druggists) normally learned their trade as apprentices. Lines were carefully drawn as to who did what job. Physicians diagnosed illnesses and prescribed treatments. They rarely soiled their hands with undignified work such as amputations, bleeding, lancing abscesses, or tooth pulling. Bloody tasks were left to surgeons—even to barbers. Mixing and selling medicines was the apothecary's realm.

In the American colonies, with so few trained doctors, Europe's rigid lines of medical status fell away. Surgeons diagnosed illnesses, apothecaries bled patients, midwives treated the sick and mixed medicines, physicians performed amputations. Doctors—being scarce—traveled a wide area visiting patients. Most medical books, and many medicines, came from Europe.

A 17th-century apothecary shop, or drugstore. The druggist's guide to medicinal plants lies open on the counter.

No matter how well a physician was trained, no matter how many books he studied, medical knowledge in the 1600s was very limited. Because churches—for centuries—had banned the dissection of human bodies, most physicians never saw the inside of a body. How the human body worked, for the most part, remained a mystery.

ONE STEP FORWARD, TWO STEPS BACK

Those physicians who defied the church to study anatomy had few tools to help them. It wasn't until the 1660s that a simple microscope, developed by Dutchman Antonj van Leeuwenhoek, opened nature's hidden world to scientists. For the first time, physicians observed tiny organisms—"wretched beasties"—swimming in water and saliva. But the fact that these "animalcules" were bacteria that could cause illness remained undiscovered.

New discoveries arrived so slowly in the study of the human body that most medical assumptions in the 1600s were based on 2,000-year-old teachings of ancient Greek physicians. For centuries, medicine focused on four bodily fluids called humors. These were blood *(sanguis),* phlegm *(pituita),* yellow bile *(chole),* and black bile *(melanchole).* They were linked to four natural elements—fire, water, air, and earth—and four conditions—hot, wet, cold, and dry. "If the Stomach be too hot," wrote one physician, "it causeth much appetite, burnt & cholerick humours, much provocation to vomit, bitter taste in the mouth."

Good health, doctors believed, depended on a balance between the four humors. Too much phlegm led to a runny nose, spitting, and fevers. Too much yellow bile caused vomiting and hot swellings. An abundance of black bile led to depression, knotty swellings, and diseases of the spleen. An excess of blood caused a strong pulse and fever.

The most common way to balance the humors was by bleeding. To remove excess blood, the physician opened a vein with a sharp knife called a lancet. For lesser cuts, the doctor used a scarificator, a metal box with small spring-loaded blades. Bleeding was usually performed near the site of the pain or the illness. "Opening of a Vein in the forehead or

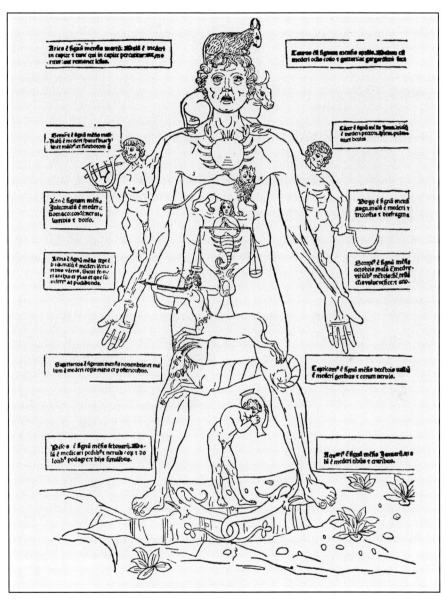

Medicine of earlier centuries was based in part on myth and misinfor-mation. For example, bleeding points on the body were thought to corre-spond to the signs of the zodiac. Bleeding a body part on the wrong day was considered dangerous.

nostrils" soothed a migraine headache. Bleeding a vein under the tongue treated a sore throat.

Bloodsucking leeches, stored in porcelain jars, were used to treat delicate areas around the eyes, mouth, and ears. Each parasite, when attached to a patient's skin, could ingest about one ounce of blood per hour, increasing its weight by as much as 800 percent. A sprinkling of salt or vinegar removed the leech from the skin.

Doctors drew humors from the body in other ways. Hot pokers, and plasters made of dried beetles, burned the skin. Excessive humors could escape through the resulting blisters. A needle and string, pulled through a pinch of skin, made another escape hole.

Patients were purged "both upward and downward" to rid the body of illness. Purging upward required an emetic, a medicine that made the patient vomit. "A spoonfull of honey, a spoonfull of fresh butter & a

Leeches sucked blood through the patient's skin.

spoonfull of clear thin Turpentine of the Pine tree is a good Vomit," recorded Thomas Palmer, a New England physician, in the late 1600s. "But one of the safest things for a Vomit is made of Radish seed, two spoonfulls" mixed with dry white wine and salad oil. "By this easy Vomit . . . many have been rid of the Cough and much Phlegm . . . I like it well. There can be no hurt in it."

Laxatives purged downward, clearing the patient's bowels. One recipe included cream of tartar and sulfur mixed with honey: "Dose in the morning; gives 2 or 3 stools." All of this purging went on, by the way, without flush toilets. Only outhouses—called privies—and chamber pots were available.

Sweating—under many blankets near a fire—also purged the body. Doctors believed that once a patient's pores opened, medicines applied as oils, ointments, and plasters would pull bad humors up through the skin.

And what if the patient failed to recover? One physician listed possible reasons: the patient did not cooperate; the patient proved unreasonable; the patient refused to pay the doctor; or sin caused the sickness, which ultimately had to be cured by God.

PHARMACOPEIA

Physicians prescribed a host of botanical medicines—made from plants and herbs; books describing botanical medicines were called herbals. Nicholas Culpeper's *Pharmacopeia Londinensis* was popular in America. Culpeper, a self-trained herbalist, offered this advice: "Have a care you use not such Medicines to one part of your body which are appropriate to another; for if your Brain be over-heated, and you use such medicines as cool the Heart or Liver, you make mad work."

Doctors scoured the countryside searching for healing plants. Home remedies came from the kitchen garden. The fouler a medicine tasted, people thought, the better it worked. The "Similars Theory," or "Doctrine of Signatures," held that "like things are cured by like things" and that every plant gave a clue to its medicinal uses. Walnut meats resembled brains and therefore were thought good for treating the head. A yellow plant, such as saffron or turmeric, treated jaundice. Plants' names also reflected treatments: sneezewort, heartsease, allheal, eyebright.

Another important medicine was cinchona bark (also called Peruvian bark because whites had learned about the drug from Peruvian Indians). It treated malaria, stomach troubles, and fevers. In 1820, a pure form of the medicine—called quinine—was isolated from the bark.

Some widely used 17th-century medicines were dangerous and addictive drugs. Opium, from the *Papaver somniferum* poppy, had been used to ease pain for thousands of years. "So necessary an instrument is opium in the hands of a skillful man, that medicine would be a cripple without it," wrote famed English physician Thomas Sydenham in 1676. But if abused, opium caused stupors, comas, and death. Laudanum, a mixture of opium, wine, and spices, was another popular painkiller.

Other painkilling drugs came from the leaves, berries, and roots of the belladona plant. But the drugs could be poisonous, and side effects included blurred vision, confusion, and hallucinations. Some soldiers at Jamestown included the plant in a salad and "turn'd natural Fools upon it for several Days." One man acted like a monkey, another blew an imaginary feather through the air, one kissed and pawed at his companions. Their drugged state took 11 days to wear off, leaving the men with no memory of what had happened.

Physicians used metals and minerals as well, including lead, sulfur, iron, and arsenic. People associated iron with strength; it was known to give "worn-out and languid blood a spur." One patient drank a syrup of iron filings, boiled with wine and sugar, for 30 days—with great improvement! (More than 200 years later, doctors learned that healthy red blood cells do require iron.)

YOU COULD SMELL A CITY FROM TEN MILES AWAY

Many people blamed sickness on "miasma," foul-smelling vapors rising from swamps and garbage piles. Americans closed their doors and windows against these vapors, afraid that the "night air" might poison and sicken them. In fact, rotting garbage could lead to sickness. But colonial

Americans didn't know why. They didn't realize that filth attracted disease-carrying insects and vermin. Swelling populations only magnified the problem.

By the end of the 1600s, America boasted several big cities. Boston was the largest, with a population of around 6,700. Colonial cities were foul-smelling places indeed! Hogs, dogs, chickens, and cows roamed the streets; carcasses often lay for days along roadsides. Horse manure clotted roads and walks. Residents tossed garbage onto the streets and threw kitchen slop near their own drinking wells. Privies stank from every yard. "Nuisance industries"—butchers, tanners, and blubber-boilers—let blood and animal parts float down the streets outside their shops. Rotting garbage bobbed in harbor waters.

Cities paid cartmen, called scavengers, to haul away debris and dead animals. But cartmen only hauled—people had to sweep and load their own garbage onto the cart. Threats of fines often failed to keep people from tossing garbage into streets and harbors. Privies were supposed to be at least 6 feet deep and at least 20 feet from a highway or house. But rules proved hard to enforce.

Towns remained home to dirt and disease, as well as growing populations. Ships sailing into colonial America's great seaside cities carried invisible cargoes of disease—disease that swept the colonies in terrible epidemics.

"WHATEVER MEASURES ARE NECESSARY"

Desperate diseases require desperate remedies.

> —Dr. Benjamin Rush,
> Philadelphia, 1793

A Brief Rule to guide the Common People of *New-England* how to Order themselves and theirs in the *Small-Pox* and *Measels*.

THE *Small Pox* (whose nature and cure the *Measels* follow) is a disease in the blood, endeavouring to recover a new form and state.

2. THIS nature attempts — 1. By Separation of the impure from the pure, thrusting it out from the Veins to the Flesh.— 2. By driving out the impure from the Flesh to the Skin.

3. THE first Separation is done in the first four Days by a Feverish boiling Ebullition) of the Blood, laying down the impurities in the Fleshy parts which kindly effected the Feverish tumult is calmed.

"In the month of February 1761 I began the study of medicine and continued constantly in my master's family and shop 'till July 1766," wrote a 15-year-old boy, apprenticed to a well-known Philadelphia physician. At the time, no medical college existed in the American colonies.

Those who could afford it trained for a year or two after apprenticeship at a medical school in Europe. Most American physicians, however, were poorly educated; some never apprenticed. Perhaps as many as four out of every five physicians had no training at all. Virtually any man could call himself a doctor and treat patients.

Newspaper editors aimed their quill pens at these "Quacks and Pretenders." One New York City paper, in 1753, called many physicians as "ignorant as boys of the lowest Class in a Reading-School." A Maryland paper noted: "The highwayman may be satisfied with your purse, while the . . . quack . . . continues to thirst after lucre [money], even at the expense of your life." The time had arrived for America to start training doctors.

As a first step, prominent physicians began offering lectures on medical topics. In 1771, Dr. Benjamin Rush, a future signer of the Declaration of Independence, advertised his talks in Philadelphia. "The whole will be taught," he promised, "in such a manner as to be intelligible to the private Gentleman and enquiring artisan, as well as the student of medicine."

Many American doctors, particularly those trained in Europe, hoped the colonies would establish a real medical school. John Morgan apprenticed in America before studying and practicing medicine in Europe for 14 years. As a member of many foreign scientific societies, including London's prestigious Royal Society, Morgan decided to return home and devote his energies to improving the medical profession in America.

Armed with letters from eminent European doctors, Morgan, along with fellow physician William Shippen, approached the trustees of the College of Philadelphia in May 1765. Would the school be interested in adding a medical department? Only the best and most eager students would be admitted—those who had finished an apprenticeship and were also educated in math, Latin, Greek, and philosophy.

The trustees agreed. America's first medical school opened its doors in November 1765 with two teachers—Morgan and Shippen. Morgan taught theory and practice of medicine, Shippen handled anatomy and surgery. If not quite up to the standards of Europe, the College of Philadelphia Medical School was a beginning.

On June 21, 1768, the school's first graduates—all 10 of them—received a "Bachelor of Physic" degree. The *Boston Chronicle* trumpeted the day "as having given birth to medical honours in America." Within

Dr. Benjamin Rush, one of the most prominent physicians in colonial America.

a few years, the school's faculty expanded. Courses included anatomy, surgery, midwifery, chemistry, practice of medicine, botany, pathology, and physiology. Lectures at Pennsylvania Hospital (America's first hospital, opened in 1752 with the support of Benjamin Franklin and other "public spirited inhabitants of Philadelphia"), let would-be doctors observe real patients. As an instructor noted, "infirmaries are the Grand Theatres of medical knowledge."

Amid festivities attended by the governor, America's second medical school opened at King's College in New York on November 2, 1767. The school boasted a faculty of six, providing "Instruction of Gentlemen in the different Branches of Medicine." With donations, and money from New York's budget, the school eventually built New York Hospital, where students could gain hands-on medical training. Following the

Revolutionary War, two more medical schools opened—at Harvard and Dartmouth.

Yet, even with these schools in operation, overall education for physicians remained poor. Few young men possessed the basic education required to attend medical school. Colleges faced a severe shortage of well-trained physicians who could serve as teachers. Most faculty members practiced medicine full-time and taught on the side. Many instructors, only in their twenties, simply read out loud the notes they'd recently scribbled down in a European lecture room.

"THE RAGE OF THE POPULACE"

With dissection frowned upon, learning was limited. Anatomy students typically pondered only wax models of the human leg or drawings of the body. One student wrote in his memoirs, "Oh if I could have had a skeleton to look at for a single hour!" When he heard about a body buried in the woods, he rushed off to examine it. "Three days hard work and work not the most pleasant. I gloated over those bones! studied them! strung them! They were the beginning of my professional knowledge."

Did some doctors resort to body snatching and grave robbing to gain medical knowledge? Yes. One Harvard student revealed that a woman's body—an old lady "both large and interestingly muscular"—was taken from Christ Church graveyard. Grave-robbing students labeled themselves "resurrectionists."

The practice fueled sentiment against doctors. When rumors spread that William Shippen had stolen bodies, a mob smashed the windows of his dissection room, while Shippen hid, afraid for his life. In September 1765, he defended himself in the newspaper: the bodies he had used were unclaimed, he declared, usually people who had killed themselves or had been publicly executed.

In March 1788, tensions over grave robbing erupted into a riot. Medical students dangled a dissected arm from a window at New York Hospital and told a boy that the arm belonged to his mother, who'd recently died. When the family checked, her grave had been disturbed. That did it! A furious crowd swarmed through the hospital, destroying classrooms. Then they turned their hostility toward physicians' offices in the city. A newspaper reported on the four days of destruction: "Our doctors by their imprudence and indecency in digging up, and exposing the dead, excited the rage of the populace." Robbing black cemeteries was tolerated, however, and African American bodies were used in many dissections.

Meanwhile, educated and conscientious physicians kept working to better their profession. John Morgan pushed for an American medical society like those in Europe, in which physicians shared knowledge and encouraged research. A few colonies did establish medical societies and attempted to keep "ignorant and unskillful persons" from practicing. In New York (beginning in 1760) and New Jersey (beginning in 1772), students had to pass an examination by a council of physicians before they could legally call themselves doctors. The regulations signaled the first round, with many ahead, in a century-long battle over licensing doctors.

MEDICINE OF THE ENVIRONMENT

In 1700, Philadelphia's population stood at 4,400. By century's end, the number had skyrocketed to 80,000. For Philadelphia and other cities, the increase in people spelled more garbage, more privies, more pollution, and more disease.

As part of the 18th century's "spirit of enlightenment," physicians, philosophers, and scientists attempted to understand and control nature. Scientists began measuring rainfall and gathering data on winds, temperature, and air pressure. Did disease occur more often in certain places? Were epidemic diseases unleashed by violent changes in the atmosphere? Certainly the miasma rising from garbage piles and marshes stank worse in warm weather. Could people avoid or even prevent the diseases expelled from a not-so-clean environment?

Community leaders pushed for an all-out attack on stagnant waters, poorly ventilated buildings, and waste-clogged streets and harbors. Citizens set about cleaning up their own yards. One woman noted in her journal that five hired men took several evenings to clean out her cesspool—a job that had not been done for 44 years. (Of course, in the absence of sewage systems and waste treatment plants, a family might clean out its privy only to dump the waste into the street in front of the house.)

People were advised to drain swamps and fill them with dirt, chop down trees, and clear away decaying garbage. Human and animal wastes, one scientist determined, were not as dangerous as rotting vegetation. Officials believed that disease could not linger if air circulated freely through buildings. So homes, jails, offices, and ships were equipped with fans and bellows. Air fresheners included simmering vinegar, burning sulfur, tar, tobacco, and gunpowder.

Before the development of indoor plumbing, people tossed wastewater outside their houses. The dirty water could contaminate drinking wells and lead to disease.

Even with such "medicine of the environment," poor sanitation remained a problem. But the cleanup resulted in improvements. People had attacked not miasma but the places where real disease carriers lived. Fleas, rats, roaches, mosquitoes, lice, flies, and bacteria fed and bred in the waters and decaying garbage piles of colonial America.

While sprucing up the environment, did people see to their own hygiene? Horrors, no. Bathing might open up the pores, they believed, inviting disease to seep into the body. And besides, lugging bathwater from a well or spring, then heating it over a fire, meant a lot of work. It was said that England's Queen Elizabeth I, who died in 1603, "took a bath once a month, if she needed it or not." One woman wrote a friend about her "shower bath": "I bore it better than I expected, not having been wett all over at once, for 28 years past." Everyone smelled, from richest to poorest, though the rich could afford perfumes and powders to mask their odors. Lice, worms, and skin conditions thrived right along with people's aversion to soap and water.

Army camps were especially filthy. During the Revolutionary War, George Washington's soldiers died more often from sickness than from British musket or cannonballs. Camp bedding and clothing, as well as contaminated water and food supplies, spread typhus, typhoid, smallpox, influenza, and dysentery. Scurvy and malnutrition decimated the troops. A Delaware physician wrote: "We lost not less than ten to twenty of camp disease for one by weapons of the enemy."

Wounded soldiers squeezed into dirty and poorly equipped hospitals. Since doctors had no medicines to fight infections, many wounds— and certainly amputations and other surgeries—usually spelled death. "Our hospital [is] crowded with 6,000 sick," wrote Benjamin Rush to Patrick Henry in January 1778, "and more dying . . . in one month than perished in the field during the whole of the last campaign." General Anthony Wayne labeled the hospital at Fort Ticonderoga a "house of carnage."

Medical officers attempted improvements. They posted rules for a healthy campsite, aired blankets, and burned used straw bedding. Dr.

Rush's book *Directions for Preserving the Health of Soldiers* was published many times, even as late as 1908. It included advice on personal hygiene, hair, shaving, clothing, tent life, and foods.

FILLING THE CHURCHYARD WITH CORPSES

The majority of Americans received medical care at home during the 1700s. Only the sickest were admitted to hospitals, regarded fearfully for many years as "the last station on the way to the grave." For most people, poor health was simply a part of everyday life.

With no refrigeration, food was often tainted. Stomach troubles were common. Cramps and diarrhea, usually caused by dysentery, were called the "bloody flux." "Fever and ague" referred to any illness with chills and fever, though recurring bouts of malaria were often the culprit. Thousands suffered from respiratory ailments such as tuberculosis, also called "consumption" because it consumed the body. The average life span in the 1700s was 35 years.

Epidemic disease—striking swiftly and viciously—was another matter entirely from daily health woes. During an epidemic, hundreds died in a short time. Disease hit without warning. Not knowing how disease spread, people trembled helplessly before the terror devastating their lives. Diphtheria, called "putrid throat distemper," struck New England in the 1730s. In one Massachusetts town, all the children in 23 families died. Boston clergyman Cotton Mather lost his wife and three of his children within two weeks. Nine hundred children died when a measles epidemic hit Charleston in 1772. In a desperate attempt to stop disease from spreading, cities often carted infected people off to pesthouses during epidemics. These squalid shelters existed only to protect the public, not to treat patients.

Colonial America's most dreaded enemy was smallpox. Victims first showed flulike symptoms, then a red rash spread across the body. The rash matured into pus-filled blisters that often left the victim's skin pitted and scarred. There was no treatment for smallpox; almost half the people who caught the disease died.

New York, 1732: "The markets begin to grow very thin; the small pox raging very violently in Town . . . which hinders the Country people from supplying this place with Provisions." Boston, 1776: Future president John Adams bemoans, "The small pox! The small pox! What shall we do with it?" City inspectors tried to quarantine ships whose sailors had smallpox. Red flags hung as a warning outside homes that sheltered patients. People scurried about their business with vinegar-soaked rags tight across their noses and mouths—protection, they hoped, from contaminated air.

But help was on the way with the greatest medical breakthrough of the 1700s—an inoculation to prevent infection. Using the tip of a quill, doctors placed pus from the blister of an infected person into a small incision on the arm of a healthy person. The healthy person developed a mild case of smallpox, from which he or she usually recovered. In response to the infection, the body developed an immunity to future exposure. Inoculation had two serious drawbacks, however. People sometimes died from the smallpox introduced by the inoculation, and they sometimes spread the disease to others.

Cotton Mather learned about smallpox inoculation from his slave Onesimus, whose African ancestors had practiced the procedure. During a 1721 smallpox outbreak, Mather put himself and his family through the process and urged fellow Bostonians to follow. Mather's push resulted in about 250 inoculations. The disease gripped Boston for a year; almost 850 people died. Only six people who'd undergone inoculation died. When smallpox struck Philadelphia in 1753, Benjamin Franklin urged fellow citizens to get inoculated. In 1777, the army began pox-proofing soldiers.

Then, in 1796, British physician Edward Jenner followed up on a local rumor that dairymaids infected with a slight case of cowpox never caught smallpox. Using the cowpox virus, Jenner began to inoculate people against smallpox. The inoculation was safe, since cowpox—a weakened strand of the pox virus—doesn't kill its victims. And with cowpox inoculation, there was no danger of an inoculated person spreading smallpox to others. Benjamin Waterhouse, a professor of medicine at Harvard, learned about Jenner's work and introduced the inoculation to the United States, where it gained rapid acceptance. Smallpox was one of the first diseases humans faced down with victory.

In August 1793, yellow fever hit Philadelphia with a vengeance. Patients suffered from high fever, vomit black with blood, and yellowed skin and eyes. A terrifying death occurred within days. Frightened people shut up their homes, smelled vinegar and camphor, chewed garlic, lit purifying fires, and shot off muskets and cannon to "agitate" the air. Thousands fled the city. Business and government came to a standstill. Other cities posted guards to block traffic from infected Philadelphia.

Volunteers and overworked physicians cared for the sick round the clock. One physician wrote that he'd hardened his heart against his patients, "otherwise I should sink under the . . . load of misery." One

During some epidemics, infected people were taken to pesthouses. Here, parents appear to be protesting as their children are put in the "smallpox van."

September week, he visited more than 100 patients per day and came home at night to find notes begging for help tacked to his door.

Taking "whatever measures are necessary to save a patient's life," Benjamin Rush gave "vigourous" medicines to yellow fever victims. He prescribed 30 grains of calomel—a drug containing poisonous mercury—and 45 grains of jalap (a laxative) daily. To counteract fever, Rush urged heavy bloodletting. "When used early on the first day," he noted, bleeding "frequently strangled the disease in its birth and generally rendered it more light."

Rush and his followers bled patients to within an inch of their lives, taking six to eight pints of blood over several days. These doctors believed that blood replenished itself in days instead of weeks. They believed the body held 12 quarts of blood instead of about 5. Some physicians, luckily for their patients, prescribed less destructive remedies: rest, wine, teas, cool baths, and "the bark"—quinine.

When the disease had run its course by late fall, nearly 5,000 people had died. Doctors debated the cause, most blaming garbage from West Indian cargo, rotting on the city's wharves. No one knew that mosquitoes, arriving with the cargo, were the real culprits. A mosquito would bite an infected person, then pass on the disease by biting someone else.

Yellow fever and other epidemics spurred American cities to pass further rules about sanitation, drainage, cleanup, and health inspections. Once the danger passed, however, laws again grew lax. People were often unwilling to pay for reforms such as new sewers and garbage removal.

SLAVERY AND SICKNESS

Black slaves suffered from the same health problems as white Americans—only worse. Forced to work outdoors in all seasons and weather, crowded into unsanitary cabins, and living on meager food supplies, African Americans suffered from many illnesses. Many slaves died two to three years after arriving on American shores.

Some slaves were immune to yellow fever and malaria. Blacks had had contact with those diseases in Africa and the West Indies and had developed some natural protection against them. But diseases unknown in Africa, such as tuberculosis, hit especially hard. Typhoid, dysentery, diphtheria, and rheumatic fever struck regularly. So too did parasites such as roundworms, threadworms, tapeworms, and hookworms. During epidemics, slaves couldn't flee the plantation for safety. One Virginia plantation lost 31 slaves to cholera in three weeks.

As a means of protecting their "property," owners did inoculate slaves against smallpox. But for most illnesses, owners first tried home remedies—cheaper than calling a doctor—or slaves tried to treat themselves. Slaves used herbal remedies and rituals handed down from memories of Africa. "Conjure doctors" removed spells from someone suddenly struck sick. Black women nursed both blacks and whites on the plantation, and large plantations had at least one black midwife. Owners earned extra money by hiring out midwives to other families.

END OF AN ERA
On December 14, 1799, as the 18th century drew to a close, America's greatest leader lay dying at his home in Virginia. Several days before, George Washington had complained of a cold and sore throat. His doctors arrived and began treatment. To ease the sore throat, they applied a mixture of blister beetles to the former president's neck. Strong laxatives purged his bowels. To "reduce the tension" in his veins and bring down his fever, they prescribed bleeding. Armed with a knife and bleeding bowl, one doctor opened a vein. Before the physicians had finished, nine pints of blood had flowed from Washington's body. America's first hero lapsed into a coma and died, killed by the "heroic treatments" meant to cure him.

"HEALTH, PURITY, AND HAPPINESS"

I wish to teach mothers how to cure their own diseases, and those of their children; and to increase health, purity, and happiness in the family and the home.

—Mary Grove Nichols,
Water Cure Journal, 1852

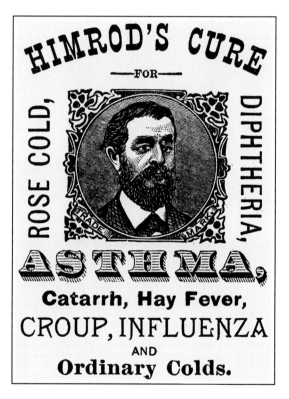

HIMROD'S CURE
—FOR—
ROSE COLD, DIPHTHERIA,
ASTHMA,
Catarrh, Hay Fever,
CROUP, INFLUENZA
AND
Ordinary Colds.

In April 1848, readers of the *United States Magazine and Democratic Review* were treated to "A Dose of Calomel," a poem by Jesse Hutchinson. While they may have laughed, many readers probably supported Hutchinson's criticism of physicians and their use of toxic remedies:

> Physicians of the highest rank,
> To pay their fees would need a bank,
> Combine all wisdom, art and skill,
> Science and sense in—*Calomel.*

The man grows worse quite fast indeed!
Go, call the doctor, ride with speed;—
The doctor comes, like post with mail,
Doubling his dose of—*Calomel.*

The man in death begins to groan,
The fatal job for him is done!
He dies alas! and sad to tell—
A sacrifice to—*Calomel.*

A backlash had begun against physicians. One 1797 attack read: "The times are ominous indeed, When quack to quack cries, purge and bleed." After Benjamin Rush's death in 1813, former president Thomas Jefferson wrote, "In his theory of bleeding and mercury, I was ever opposed to my friend Rush, whom I greatly loved; but who has done much harm, in the sincerest persuasion that he was preserving life."

By the thousands, people turned away from bloodletting and purges and embraced gentler remedies. Believing a strong body less vulnerable to disease, Americans vigorously pursued good nutrition and exercise, fresh air, sunshine, and herbal medicines. Dr. Oliver Wendell Holmes (1809–1894) scorned the idea as "nature-trusting heresy," but many people had faith that they could care for themselves as well as, if not better than, trained physicians could.

"EVERY MAN HIS OWN PHYSICIAN"

Instead of calomel and the lancet, Samuel Thomson offered his followers "fruitful fields, green pastures, and flowery banks . . . to gather roots, and leaves, and blossoms, barks and fruits, for . . . healing." Largely uneducated, Thomson learned about botanical medicine from an old neighbor woman who treated locals with plants and herbs. By 1809 he'd set himself up as a traveling doctor, taking on patients much to the anger of area physicians. When one of his patients died, Thomson faced charges of manslaughter and medical malpractice. The court found him innocent, and Thomson continued to push his remedies.

In 1813 he obtained a patent on his system of medical treatment and went into business, selling his vision with the motto: Every Man His Own Physician. For $20, families received a kit full of instructions and numbered glass bottles of herbal medicines. Treatments, which included steaming a patient near a fireplace or stove, reflected the basic notion: "let nature take its course."

Other doctors learned Thomson's techniques. One follower claimed that one-sixth of Boston's population in 1828 relied on a Thomson-trained doctor. During the high point of interest in Thomson's methods, around 1840, an estimated three million families dispensed treatments from his home medical kit.

People also bought do-it-yourself medical handbooks. *Dr. Gunn's Domestic Medicine* promised "any man unless he was a fool or an idiot, could amputate an arm or leg, provided he had half a dozen men to hold the victim down." Mary S. Bosley offered a wide range of helpful advice in her *Handbook on Useful Knowledge, Comprising a Valuable Selection of Recipes in Medicines, Choice Things in Cookery, New Ideas in Gardening, etc., etc.*

By the 1840s, homeopathy, a practice based on the old idea that "like cures like," was on the rise. What medicine would give a healthy person symptoms similar to those that afflicted the patient? A homeopath might treat a case of diarrhea with a small dose of laxative. Homeopaths used mostly gentle, botanical treatments, given in small or diluted doses.

Health movements and quackish cures also flourished. Some people followed the "Gospel of Relaxation," others joined the "Don't Worry Movement." Another group advised dressing each morning while chanting: "Youth, Health, Vigor!" Some people turned to hypnotism to cure their ills. Electricity—newly understood and harnessed—was used to treat everything from cancer to dysentery, consumption, and blindness. One entrepreneur convinced hundreds that his metallic fork, with one steel and one brass tine, cured illness. Some people still viewed bleeding as healthful. *The Planter's Guide and Family Book of Medicine* (1849) gave step-by-step instructions on how to bleed a patient. One West

Virginia history book from 1891 states: "In fact, it was the rule, to be bled every spring, just after maple sugar making."

Hydrotherapy, "the water cure," involved dipping, dunking, bathing, and hosing, as well as drinking water. Cereal maker John Harvey Kellogg was a supporter, along with Mary Grove Nichols, a contributor to the *Water Cure Journal,* read by more than 10,000 women. Addressing health concerns of women and children, Nichols offered advice on subjects from teething to bathing to women's clothing. She criticized hoopskirts, corsets, and heavy petticoats that restricted movement and cut off breath. "We can expect but small achievement from women," she wrote in 1850, "so long as it is the labor of their lives to carry about their clothing."

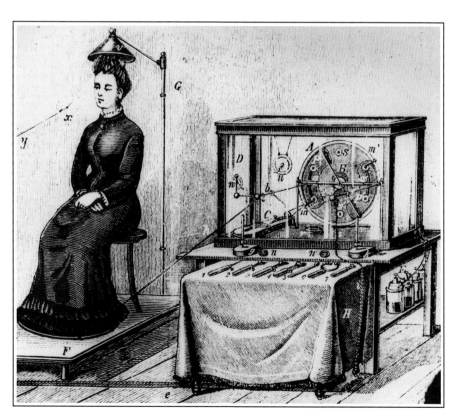

A system for treating headaches with electricity

Wealthy women during the 1800s were often viewed as frail and fragile. Some spent a good deal of time lying in bed or on the sofa, sometimes drugged with laudanum or opium prescribed for headaches and "female complaints." (Middle-class and poor women rarely took such "cures." They had too much work to do.) Female health reformers, meanwhile, urged women to stop being "puny, sickly, aching, weakly, dying" creatures and to "throw off the shackles that have hitherto bound both body and mind, and rise into the newness of life."

In 1875, Mary Baker Eddy published *Science and Health, with the Key to the Scriptures.* Sickly as a child, Eddy believed that medical treatment further weakened the body. She founded the Church of Christian Science, based on the philosophy that the mind has powers to heal the body with prayer. Other religious groups denounced "doctors, drugs, and devils." Faith healers claimed God-given powers to cure with prayers and the touch of their hands.

INSIDE THE FAMILY MEDICINE CHEST

Most families kept remedies on hand like quinine, some form of opium, and whiskey—grabbed for most ailments. Purges included calomel (one book touted: "perhaps, no medicine is more generally useful than this") and castor oil. Also on hand were camphor, liniments, peppermint essence, herbal teas, and "physicking" pills. If a medicine tasted strong and bitter, it was thought to provide a good cure.

Many harmless mixtures had no value at all. Other medicines, though downright dangerous and addictive, made patients in pain feel better. Such cure-alls as Turlington's Balsam of Life, Ma Munn's Elixir of Opium, and Dr. Ryan's Worm Destroying Sugar Plums treated the family at home. Dr. Ryan's medicine was advertised as "one of the best purges in the world for gross bodied children that are apt to breed worms . . . mild, safe and pleasant; [the plums] wonderfully cleanse the bowels of all stiff and clammy humours, which stop up the parts."

Lydia Pinkham's Vegetable Tonic For Female Problems, a household staple in the mid-1800s, was 18 percent alcohol. Pinkham's tonic was so

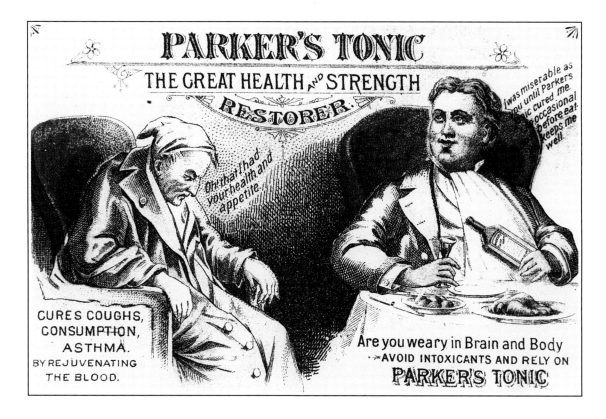

popular that some small-town newspapers used her face off the label to illustrate articles calling for a female portrait. Once, she even served as a stand-in for England's Queen Victoria.

Some medicines, like belladonna and laudanum, could bring tragic results. As a child in 1846, Lucy Henderson Deady traveled west on the Oregon Trail with her family. She later recalled:

> Mother had brought some medicine along. . . . My little sister, Salita Jane wanted to taste it. . . . as soon as we had gone she got the bottle and drank it all. Presently she came to the campfire where Mother was cooking supper and said she felt awfully sleepy. . . . When Mother tried to awake her later she couldn't arouse her. Lettie had drunk the whole bottle of laudanum. It was too late to save her life.

Medicines with such helpful-sounding names as Mrs. Winslow's Soothing Syrup, A Pennysworth of Peace, and Mother Bailey's Quieting Syrup were regularly used by mothers to quiet fussy infants and children. They did the trick all right—all contained a form of opium.

Americans flocked to medicine shows, circuslike promotional stunts used to sell remedies—supposedly based on Native American recipes.

This 19th-century lithograph shows "Dr. M. A. Simmons selling his liver medicine on the American frontier." Many so-called cures were ineffective—even harmful.

Shows featured Indians performing "war dances" and generally lending an air of the Wild West. White Americans believed Indians lived a robust and healthy life. So Native American medicines must be superior, customers thought. Labels were decorated with warbonneted chiefs and Indian maidens. Nez Perce Catarrh Snuff, Old Sachem Bitters, War Paint Ointment, Wigwam Tonic, and Seminole Cough Balsam read but a few. In fact, the medicines had nothing to do with Indian remedies. Most bottles contained drugs from pharmaceutical companies and large doses of alcohol. Many quack physicians rode the same wave, promoting themselves as "Indian doctors" who had learned medical secrets while living among the Indians.

"TO WHOOP AND ENJOY LIFE"

In March 1832, Charles Caraway wrote to his family in Virginia from his new western home in Illinois. "I have enjoyed as good health since I have lived here as I ever have in the same length of time," he exclaimed. He urged other family members to move west to better land, better health. But other midwesterners found that the Ohio and Mississippi river valleys raged with disease in summer—yellow fever, malaria, aches, and sweats.

Reports from the Far West sounded better. "There was but one man in California that had ever had a shake," claimed an 1840 report, "it was a matter of much wonderment." "Let a man travel 6 weeks in western Texas," came another story, "and if he is not cured . . . of whatever ailment he has, it will be because there is no blood left in him." Author Mark Twain noted these observations near Lake Tahoe on the Nevada-California border:

> I know a man who went there to die. But he made a failure of it. He was a skeleton when he came, and could barely stand. . . . Three months later he was sleeping out of doors . . . eating all he could hold . . . and chasing over mountains. . . . And he was a skeleton no longer. I confidently commend his experience to other skeletons.

Read, Reason & REFLECT!

DR. PARMENTER'S
MAGNETIC OIL!
Will Cure Rheumatism!

TO THOSE AFFLICTED!

This Oil is warranted to ease more pain in less time, than any other medicine now in use. Call and test its Virtue; it removes the worst Rheumatic pain in 30 minutes; pains in the side, breast and back, in 20 minutes; Nervous Headache in 10 minutes; Croup in 20 minutes; Chilblains in one night, and is a sure cure for chapped hands. The Oil acts on the System on the principle of Electricity, regulates the whole system, and is perfectly safe in all cases. **PRICE 25 CENTS PER BOTTLE.**

PRINCIPAL DEPOT,
No. 9 Cooper's Buildings, cor. State & Green Sts.,
ALBANY, N. Y., and for sale by Druggists generally, throughout the United States and the Canadas. Druggists, Merchants and Peddlers supplied at the lowest prices,

By Dr. WM. O. PARMENTER.

BAKER TAYLOR, PRINTER, 9 STATE STREET, ALBANY.

The pure, fresh air of western lands specifically lured consumptives. Tuberculosis patients arrived by the thousands to settle for good or to live in tent cities while taking "the cure" for three or four months. A steady stream of invalids poured thousands of dollars into sanitariums and health resorts in Colorado, New Mexico, California, and Arizona. Colorado was dubbed "The World's Sanitarium." Not to be left behind, an Arizona physician in 1893 noted that his area had "no dews, no fogs, no rapid changes from heat to cold, no decaying vegetation, no rivers, pools, or lakes germinating poisonous miasmas."

Western waters and hot springs were said to supply cure-alls. "There are springs all about," claimed a Texan, "which possess a whole apothecaryship of medical qualities." Alkaline waters allegedly treated malaria and tuberculosis. Saline waters were said to improve gout. Sulfur waters were used to aid liver problems, respiratory ailments, and skin disease. One success story, even among a hundred failures, was all it took to keep consumptive, sickly easterners traveling west.

"NEAR THE HOUR OF LABOR"

One August morning in 1787, Martha Ballard began her day before dawn. "I am at Mrs. Howards watching with her son," she wrote in her journal. She continued:

> Left James Exceeding Dangerously ill . . . to Joseph Fosters to see her sick children. Find Saray and Daniel very ill. Came home went to the field & got some Cold Water root. Then calld to Mr. Kenydays to see Polly. Very ill with the Canker [scarlet fever]. Gave her some of the root. I gargled her throat which gave her great ease. Returned home after dark.

Ballard was a midwife in Maine. She delivered 816 newborns during her career, although—as her journal shows—she did much more than deliver babies. She made and dispensed medicine, diagnosed and treated illnesses, purged and bled patients. If necessary, she prepared bodies for burial. Ballard even witnessed several autopsies.

Often, people paid Ballard in goods instead of money. Her ledger listed payments of salt, white rum, sugar, and spices. She usually charged two dollars for delivering a baby. The town's doctor received six dollars for the same service.

Midwife and doctor were not always in agreement. In one instance, a doctor gave one of Ballard's patients 20 drops of laudanum, which put the woman into such a stupor that her "regular and promising" labor pains stopped. When the doctor delivered a stillborn baby, Ballard called him a "poor, unfortunate man in the practice." A month later, he gave up a case to Ballard, who safely delivered the baby.

But times were changing for midwives. Male physicians saw that money could be made in the area of women's health care. Although poor women continued delivering babies at home with a midwife assisting, by 1800 it was fashionable for wealthier women to be attended by a male doctor during childbirth. *The Midwives Monitor and Mother's Mirror*, printed in 1800, told women they knew very little about childbirth. In 1820, a Harvard medical professor declared, "a female could scarce pass through the course of education requisite to prepare her, as she ought to be prepared, for the practice of midwifery."

But doctors who handled sick patients and dead bodies before delivering babies unknowingly passed on infection. Ironically, as women began going to hospitals for their babies' births, death rates for mothers and infants climbed.

Oppposite: Midwife Sibby Kelly, born a slave, delivered babies well into the 20th century.

"GENTLEMEN, THIS IS NO HUMBUG!"

The astonishing claim had been made that it would render the person operated upon free from pain.

—Washington Ayer,
eyewitness account of ether
demonstration, October 16, 1846

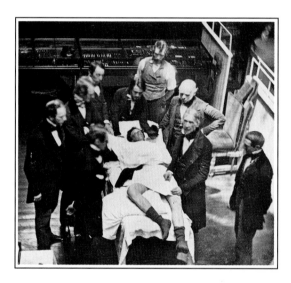

In 1793, Harvard Medical School required entering students to have completed an apprenticeship with a reputable doctor and to have had a basic education in Latin, philosophy, and math. Harvard students attended lectures in anatomy, theory and practice of medicine, chemistry, and *materia medica* (Latin for medical materials). Before receiving their degrees, students faced a grilling by professors and members of the Massachusetts Medical Society.

Nearly 100 years later, the situation at Harvard was very different. A student could fail final examinations in four branches of medical science and still become a doctor. James Clarke White, who later taught medicine at Harvard, remembered his single question on the surgery exam. "Well, White," he was asked, "what would you do for a wart?"

"A few months' attendance at lectures," complained an 1876 editorial in the *New York Daily Tribune,* "a sham examination, and the vulgar

quacks . . . are turned out, thousands at a time, licensed to kill or cure."
A professor at Saint Louis College of Physicians and Surgeons protested
that students took only "two short terms of four months each," then "a
final examination of head and pocket; for there is a parting fee of twenty-
five dollars demanded for a diploma, which, if written in Latin, not one
percent of the graduates can translate into Fair English." One paper
called it a joke to speak of medicine "as one of the learned professions."
In 1831 the *North American Review* declared, "Physicians are . . . made
the butt of ridicule, and not unfrequently the subject of sweeping and
unsparing censure."

Between 1830 and 1850, most states repealed laws requiring doctors
to pass an exam and earn a license before setting up shop. Americans,
nourished on freedom, frowned on regulations of any type. But without
licensing, quacks and poorly trained doctors overran the country. Anyone "learned or ignorant, an honest man or a knave, can assume the

*In this English cartoon, the doctors in charge of testing new surgeons are
either sleeping, counting their money, or similarly distracted.*

name of physician, and 'practice' upon anyone, to cure or to kill, as either may happen, without accountability. It's a free country!" a New York physician lamented in 1838.

Under such criticism, doctors actively fought to save their profession. From every state echoed calls for reform. But who would decide what was needed? Not the government, cried one medical group, for "to trust to politicians for the advancement of scientific medicine would be to seek . . . such protection as wolves give to lambs."

In May 1846, delegates from 16 states met in New York to study the medical profession in the United States. Committees formed to look into problems, mail surveys to medical schools, and set up another convention for the following year. This first step taken by the newly formed American Medical Association (AMA) foreshadowed future problems: 10 states didn't bother to send delegates to the meeting and only one-third of the nation's medical colleges had someone in attendance.

The AMA pushed for higher standards: Incoming medical students would need proof that they'd completed a well-rounded preliminary education. At least three years of medical school would be required. Each year, students would have to take specific courses and pass exams before moving ahead to the next level. Every student would have to perform at least three months of dissection and hospital work. Schools would have to have at least one instructor for each branch of medicine.

Supporters hoped that these rules would erect a barrier "against the disgraceful practice of conferring the distinguished title of Doctor of Medicine upon men so illiterate that they cannot write an ordinary business letter in creditable English." Reform was finally underway.

"BEGINNING TO PINE FOR MORE KNOWLEDGE"

In November 1847, a young woman dressed in hoopskirts and a bonnet walked into a classroom at Geneva College in western New York. Elizabeth Blackwell (1821–1910) had studied medical books and apprenticed for two years with practicing physicians. But her applications to 28 medical schools had all been rejected.

Then came a day of great joy when Geneva College accepted her as the first female medical student in the country. Unfortunately, the all-male student body had only voted to admit Blackwell as a joke. They never dreamed she'd actually show up. Blackwell not only showed up, she stayed to face hostility from classmates and professors who barred her from laboratories and sometimes even lectures. In 1849, Blackwell graduated at the top of her class, the first female physician trained at college.

Women had always served as healers. But the men in charge of higher education thought that women were too "irrational," "hysterical," and lacking in courage to advance in the field of medicine. Too much education deformed women, the men claimed, producing "monstrous brains and puny bodies." Nor could a woman's "tender nature" bear the blood, gore, and mysteries of the human body. A Harvard medical professor noted in 1820: "It is obvious that we cannot instruct women as we do men in the science of medicine; we cannot carry them into the dissecting room and the hospital." When Harriet Hunt tried to enter Harvard Medical School in the late 1840s, the senior class protested that her "presence is calculated to destroy our respect for the modesty and delicacy of her sex."

Elizabeth Blackwell

During those early days, women in medicine wove together a small network to help and support one another. Elizabeth Blackwell's sister Emily (1826–1910) was rejected by 11 medical schools before finishing her education at Western Reserve University in Cleveland. The school also accepted another female student, Marie Zakrzewska, a German immigrant.

Because most hospitals and clinics refused to employ female physicians, Elizabeth Blackwell, with the aid of some Quaker friends, founded the New York Infirmary for Women and Children in 1857. The hospital's all-female staff included doctors Emily Blackwell and Marie Zakrzewska.

"EASING HUMAN SUFFERING"

On October 16, 1846, at Massachusetts General Hospital, Gilbert Abbott lay upon a wooden table and inhaled ether vapors from a glass bottle until he fell unconscious. Dr. John Warren quickly stepped forward and cut away a tumor on the left side of Abbott's neck and jaw. Spectators watched and waited. No screams erupted from the patient. Had Abbott survived? If so, had he felt pain? Slowly, Abbott awoke and when questioned replied that he'd suffered no pain and remembered nothing of the surgery.

Dr. Warren turned to the others in the room and announced his experiment with anesthesia a success. "Gentlemen," he declared, "this is no humbug." The discovery of anesthesia, from the Greek words "without feeling," was one of the greatest steps forward in medical science.

The first two anesthetics, nitrous oxide (laughing gas) and ether, were already known to the public through "frolics." Soaking a cloth with ether and inhaling the vapors for "exhilarating effects" became quite fashionable. People staggered about and behaved oddly, crashing and falling down, while spectators enjoyed a good laugh.

Crawford Williamson Long of Georgia attended ether parties and noticed the next day many painful bruises and scrapes he had no recollection of receiving. He figured they must have happened under the influence of ether. Surely, these injuries would have caused pain in a person not in a state of anesthesia.

In 1842, Long began testing his conclusions. Patients inhaled ether vapor from a towel while Long performed surgeries: removing a cyst, amputating a toe. Long's experiments were probably the first purposeful use of anesthetics, but he did not publish a paper about his feat until 1848. By then, others—such as Warren—had already proven the point.

Dr. William Morton noted that different operations required different amounts of ether. He recorded that after a patient breathed ether vapors for three minutes:

> The pulse is quickened and the muscles relaxed, so that the head . . . falls on one side, the patient should be told, in a loud, distinct tone, to open his eyes; and, if he does not do so, the operation should be immediately commenced. If he does open his eyes, even in a slow and languid manner, he should be directed to close them, and the inhalation should be continued two minutes longer, when the same question may be repeated; and it will usually be found that, by this time, the patient is unconscious.

Dentist Horace Wells first used nitrous oxide in 1844 to extract teeth from unconscious patients. Toothache had previously been treated by inserting opium or another medicine in the cavity of a decaying tooth. When that failed, diseased teeth were yanked, twisted, or pried out of their sockets. Sometimes the dentist or surgeon held the poor sufferer down with a knee to the chest for better leverage. Legions of patients cheered anesthesia as the great blessing of dentistry.

Prior to the 19th century, people had few ways to relieve pain besides taking opium or drinking alcohol to the point of oblivion. Early in the century, scientists isolated different elements from opium and created more painkilling drugs. One of these was morphine, named after Morpheus, the Greek god of sleep. Another drug was codeine. From morphine came heroin, which was highly addictive and dangerous. Later discoveries were cocaine and novocaine.

Physicians injected medicine directly beneath the skin using "the Painful Point"—a syringe—better known as a shot. A glass tube marked

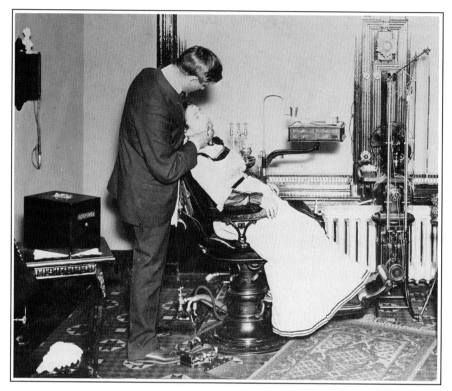

By the mid-19th century, thanks to anesthetics such as nitrous oxide, patients no longer dreaded visits to the dentist.

with measurements held the medicine. A plunger, "being shoved home," delivered the dose through a hollow needle. Since 1858, the syringe has stayed basically the same. Painkillers injected directly into tissue, muscles, or veins, could relieve people's suffering within moments.

Other new tools arrived from Europe. In 1816, a stout young woman showing symptoms of heart disease consulted French physician René Laënnec. In most cases, doctors listened to the heart by placing an ear on the patient's chest, a method used since the days of ancient Greece. Too embarrassed to use this method, the Frenchman rolled tight a piece of paper and placed one end over the woman's heart. At the other end, he listened.

"I was both surprised and gratified," he recalled, "at being able to hear the beating of the heart with much greater clearness and distinctness than I had ever done before by direct application of my ear. I at once saw that this means might become a useful method for studying, not only the beating of the heart, but likewise all movements [of the inner body] capable of producing sound." Laënnec had invented the stethoscope.

The English translation of Laënnec's work on the stethoscope, and his findings on heart and lung disease, appeared in the United States in 1823. Most physicians embraced the new tool, but one professor of medicine warned doctors that they needed to use common sense as well. In an 1849 poem, he told the tale of a young doctor fooled into a wrong diagnosis by two flies trapped under his stethoscope:

> Now use your ears, all that you can,
> But don't forget to mind your eyes,
> Or you may be cheated, like this young man,
> By a couple of silly, abnormal flies.

MEDICAL CALAMITIES

An 1848 issue of the *Pittsburgh Daily Gazette* told the tale of a young woman contemplating suicide. She jumped into a local canal but, "beholding its filthy condition, and inhaling its foetid odor, she concluded to postpone drowning until she could meet with cleaner water."

Indeed, waterways were foul in 19th-century cities and could kill by methods other than drowning. Cholera bacteria spread through contaminated water. The infection violently dehydrated the victim's body through diarrhea, vomiting, and fever. For most, death was swift—sometimes within hours.

In the late 1840s, cholera swept across Europe—from Russia to Germany to England. Newspaper reports informed Americans as the terror crept closer to home. Finally, in December 1848, a ship from Europe carried the disease into New York City. Though people tried many remedies—from laudanum to hot pepper sauce—nothing worked. By May, 5,000 Americans had died.

From 1848 until 1854, the dreaded illness was America's constant enemy. The disease spread along the Ohio River. It entered the port of New Orleans, crept up the Mississippi River to St. Louis, and from there joined western-bound pioneers on the Oregon Trail. Hundreds of emigrants shared campsites, tainted water supplies, and death. Some wagon trains lost two-thirds of their people. Emigrants counted the weary miles by recording grave markers standing stark along the roadside.

Then, beginning in 1861, the country faced an even greater medical disaster. The Civil War ripped the nation in two—North against South. Crowded into dirty camps and hospitals, soldiers died not only of battle wounds but also of disease, poor nutrition, and exposure. Dysentery and "fever and ague" marched alongside armies. Wrote one northern doctor, "The army is decimated by sickness every day."

A Union soldier offers water to a wounded comrade.

Battles amounted to living nightmares. Surgeons operated for hours at a time on the wounded while bullets whistled overhead. Many times, after long days treating their own men, doctors treated helpless casualties from the enemy side. As battle lines shifted, hospital tents were ripped down, the wounded hurried into ambulance wagons, supplies gathered helter-skelter.

On May 5, 1863, a young Union doctor named William Watson scribbled a few words to his father from the Chancellorsville battlefield: "We were compelled to move Division Hospital five times—being shelled out. The first Hospital was knocked to pieces five minutes after we got out . . . I have been operating a great deal. Don't know how many amputations I have performed."

A few days later, he lashed out at three fellow physicians who "ran off over the river in the first day's fight and never came back at all." He continued: "I know many of the wounded who came to Division Hospital had not their wounds dressed for six, some even for ten days—and the gangrene and maggots resulted from this neglect. For the sake of humanity I want to see [the physicians] punished."

At Gettysburg, Pennsylvania, Watson performed 14 amputations in a barn riddled with flying bullets without once moving from the operating table. "Most of the wounded are lying on the wet ground without any shelter whatever," he wrote. He stayed at Gettysburg for two months, reporting that "the mortality among the wounded is fearful. Most of the cases die." Sometimes the ratio of patients to medical officers was 700 to 3.

President Abraham Lincoln, ultimately leading the North to victory, pledged to "bind up the nation's wounds." But when the fighting finally stopped, more than 600,000 soldiers had lost their lives. Weary Americans mourned their dead and returned to peacetime pursuits.

Doctors turned from binding the wounds of war to improving their own profession. The United States was a growing country, a magnet for immigrants, home to industry and sprawling cities. Could the medical profession keep pace with the nation's changes?

PHYSICIAN, HEAL THYSELF

The time for reform has assuredly arrived—the cry for it comes from all parts of the country.

—Daniel Drake,
physician, 1840

The "scourge of the human race." The White Plague. Consumption. TB. By any name, tuberculosis spread alarmingly in the the second half of the 19th century. "Of 75,000,000 living Americans, 8,000,000 at least must inevitably die from this cause," one magazine reported. "Some authorities put the estimate as high as 10,000,000."

Tuberculosis hit especially hard among the crush of new immigrants to America's cities and mining towns in the late 19th century. The bacteria thrived in the immigrants' crowded, poorly ventilated, dirty tenement homes. Underfed and overworked, factory workers and miners were easy prey for TB germs. Yellow fever epidemics also blazed during summer months, striking hardest in the South. In 1879, 16,000 people died of yellow fever in just a few months.

As in previous centuries, epidemics prompted cries to clear away garbage, clean up water supplies, ventilate buildings, and construct sewer systems. This work, accompanied by advances in medical knowledge, went a long way toward improving health. But physicians and their patients still had a lot to learn.

ANTISEPTIC CLEAN

Although anesthesia had revolutionized surgery in the 1840s, half of all surgery patients died of infections after operations. Some physicians suspected that scrubbing their hands would keep disease from spreading between patients. Other doctors ridiculed the idea.

In surgical theaters, doctors and students could observe operations and other medical procedures.

In the 1860s, French chemist Louis Pasteur showed that bacteria—living organisms so small they could only be seen under a microscope—caused killer infections in wounds and surgical incisions. Joseph Lister, in Edinburgh, Scotland, realized the importance of Pasteur's work and wondered whether chemicals could be used to destroy bacteria on wounds and medical equipment.

In August 1865, Lister used a carbolic acid spray to disinfect his operating room. His theory proved a lifesaver. Other physicians followed Lister's lead. Using antiseptics like iodine, they cleaned operating rooms, instruments, bandages, even their own clothing. More patients began to survive difficult surgeries.

In July 1893, a young man stabbed in the chest was quickly failing. Daniel Hale Williams, trained at Howard University (founded in 1868 as a medical school for African Americans), suspected the man's heart had been cut. The only way to save him was to open the chest and attempt surgery on the heart. Williams made an incision and cut away a tiny portion of the man's rib. Inside, a major blood vessel had been nicked. Williams tied it off, stopping the bleeding. The sack around the heart was torn, too. Struggling to work while the sack fluttered with every heartbeat, Williams stitched the wound closed. At each step, he cleaned the wound. By the end of the surgery, the young physician was dripping with sweat. As the next days unfolded, the patient improved. After 51 days, Williams sent him home. One newspaper headline summed up Williams' pioneering work: "Sewed Up His Heart!"

THE TIME FOR REFORM

As scientific research gathered speed like a boulder crashing downhill, the need for reform at medical schools became more and more apparent. But year after year passed without progress. The AMA pressured colleges to make changes. In the late 1860s, the association decided to "recognize" colleges that followed its reform guidelines and to condemn schools that didn't. Harvard, under President Charles Eliot, was one of the schools that complied. Upgraded requirements for medical students

An unregulated medical school in Topeka, mid-19th century

included three years of study, terms of nine months, and oral and written exams in each department.

The result? Over the next several years, Harvard's medical school enrollment plummeted by 43 percent. Other schools promised students a degree in just two years, with only four-month terms. Without every medical college raising its standards, reform seemed doomed. As one doctor put it, if reform was the prescription, "either the pill prepared has been too big for the throat, or the throat too constricted for the pill."

Meanwhile, scandal surfaced. Beginning in 1870, a man named John Buchanan had printed and sold more than 60,000 medical diplomas from the American College of Medicine in Pennsylvania. In 1880 reporters exposed the scam. Buchanan was sent to prison, but other diploma mills kept operating. When the Illinois Board of Health began

*Some people viewed
doctors as incompetent—
even dangerous—
"quacks."*

to examine and license doctors, it discovered that from 1877 to 1879, 10 percent of the state's physicians had simply bought their diplomas through the mail.

People began to realize that licensing doctors would protect the public. If every state required licenses, poorly qualified doctors couldn't vamoose to other states with lax laws. When Illinois set up a state licensing board, as many as one-quarter of its physicians either failed the medical test or fled the state.

In 1879, only 7 out of 38 states had effective licensing laws. A physician from New Orleans offered these judgments: Connecticut, no legal restrictions; Kansas, "the most ignorant pretender may dub himself a doctor;" Missouri, "overrun with quacks." In Louisiana, the physician's home state, the tax collector issued medical licenses to anyone who paid $20.

By 1893, the situation had improved. Twenty-three states had licensing laws. New York even had separate boards to examine ordinary doctors, homeopathic physicians, and eclectics—who borrowed practices from several types of physicians.

A MODEL UNIVERSITY

In 1876 Johns Hopkins University, endowed by a wealthy banker and railroad stockholder, was founded in Baltimore. With an endowment, the university was not dependent on student fees for its success. From the start, Johns Hopkins hired well-trained physicians as instructors— many educated in Germany. These men lectured less and demonstrated more. Most were full-time teachers and researchers, not practicing physicians who taught on the side.

Students faced a four-year program and extensive laboratory work. Third- and fourth-year students worked in hospital wards and assisted with surgery. Johns Hopkins delivered a revolution in medical education. Gone was the old idea of "reading medicine." The new idea—practicing medicine. Within 20 years, more than 60 colleges had three or more professors with a degree from prestigious Johns Hopkins. The school's innovative ideas spread.

Not all qualified students were welcome at Johns Hopkins and other medical colleges. Women and minorities were usually shunned from the ranks. Out of necessity, African American and female doctors formed their own schools, hospitals, and medical societies. Nearly 100 black hospitals operated by 1910. In 1868, Elizabeth Blackwell opened a medical college for women, providing clinical work at her hospital, tough exams, and a strict course of study. In 1884, Mary Hobart graduated from Blackwell's school. As a graduation gift, she received a family treasure, the diary of her great-great-grandmother—midwife Martha Ballard.

Marie Zakrzewska, "Dr. Zak," eventually left the New York Infirmary and moved to Boston, where she founded the New England Hospital for Women and Children in 1862. Her nursing program graduated the first African American nurse, Mary Mahoney. After being turned down many times for acceptance into the Massachusetts Medical Society, Dr. Zak declined the honor when it was finally granted to her in 1884.

By 1897, 50 years after Elizabeth Blackwell made history, almost 7,000 women had earned medical degrees. Stressing good hygiene and nutrition, female physicians visited city slums and tried to educate mothers on how to raise healthy children. However, male doctors felt that too many women had entered the profession. More and more women began to see their medical school applications rejected.

By 1900, all but 3 of 19 women's medical schools established during the 1800s had closed or been incorporated into men's medical colleges. The number of female medical students also began slipping. In 1896,

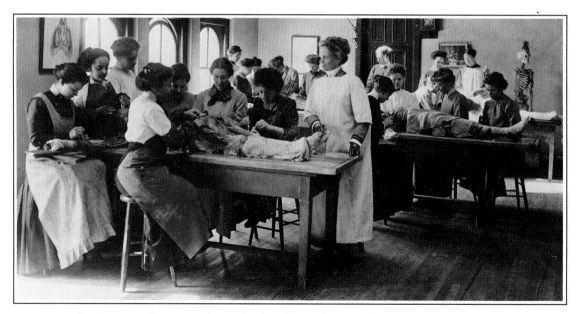

Students at the Women's Medical College of Pennsylvania dissect cadavers, around 1900.

33 percent of Johns Hopkins graduates were women. By 1910 that number had dropped to three percent. Many hospitals wouldn't hire female graduates.

In this unfriendly climate, many women channeled their healing abilities into nursing, which society viewed as a more "womanly" calling. But nurses were expected to keep their "proper station"; a nurse was not to invade the doctor's realm. A 1901 article in the *Journal of the American Medical Association* chided the nurse who was "too unconscious of the due subordination she owes to the medical profession, of which she is sort of a useful parasite."

The largest hospitals and medical schools established nurse training programs. Student nurses worked 12 hours a day, without pay except for a room and food. After graduation, most nurses cared for the sick in private homes instead of hospitals. Through home visits, especially to the poor, public health department nurses provided the first—and sometimes only—health care to many American children.

Isabel Hampton, superintendent of Johns Hopkins Nursing School, organized the first meeting of the National League of Nursing Education, which in 1896 became the American Nurses' Association. The *American Journal of Nursing* began publishing in 1900. Eight years later, the AMA recognized nurses as members of the medical profession.

BIG CHANGES AT LAST

The AMA kept the pressure on inferior medical schools. By 1900 it decided that any college with less than a four-year program could not send delegates to yearly AMA meetings. The AMA's Council on Medical Education began rating colleges according to the percentage of their students who failed state board exams. Ratings ranged from A+ to C−. Most states refused to license graduates of class-C schools. The message: reform or go out of business.

In 1908 Abraham Flexner, working for the Carnegie Foundation, scrutinized America's medical colleges and recommended that the system undergo a complete overhaul. He called for reducing the number of colleges

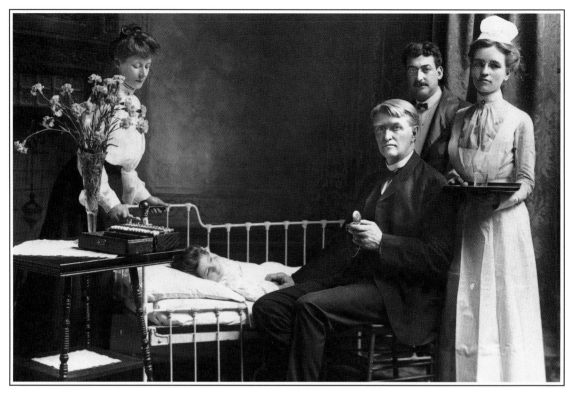

In this photograph from the late 19th century, both a doctor and a nurse visit a sick child at home. Doctors continued to make house calls until the mid-20th century.

from 155 to 31. Each school should be a department of a larger university, he said, and located in a large city with hospital work available. He recommended specialized, full-time instructors and four years of high school and two years of college as prerequisites for students. As a result of Flexner's reports, many schools closed. "The weak schools in all sections of the country . . . have been almost wholly eliminated," he noted.

By the 1920s, America's haphazard system of training physicians had been swept aside. Only the brightest and best-prepared students were admitted to medical schools. Only the sharpest could hope to understand and master the new advances being made around the world in chemistry and bacteriology. Between 1879 and 1900, scientists identified 21 different disease-causing bacteria, including those that caused diphtheria, typhoid, dysentery, and plague. In 1882, researchers learned that the bite of the anopheles mosquito spread malaria.

By the 1880s, upper-class Americans had begun to install plumbing systems and flush toilets inside their houses. (Many poor and rural Americans wouldn't enjoy such conveniences until decades later.) Cities began building waterworks—systems for supplying clean water to homes and businesses—and sewers for carrying wastewater away.

The renewed emphasis on cleanliness, and advances such as x rays (1895), ushered in big changes. People began living longer. The average life expectancy from 1800 to 1850 had been about 40 years. By 1900 most people could expect to live to about 50. In 1800 half of all American children died before age five. In 1900 the odds were better: only one out of every four children died. And more medical breakthroughs were right around the corner.

A BRIGHT HORIZON

Victory Against Polio! Salk's Vaccine Works.

> —*Chicago Tribune,*
> April 12, 1955

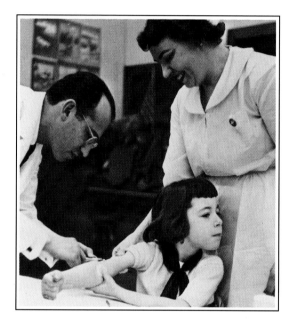

In 1906 Upton Sinclair's novel *The Jungle* hit Americans, literally, in the stomach. The novel exposed the life of immigrant laborers in the stock-yards, where animals were slaughtered and processed to make food. At breakfast one morning, President Theodore Roosevelt ate while he read:

> There was never the least attention paid to what was cut up for sausage . . . old sausage that . . . was moldy and white . . . meat on the floor, in the dirt and sawdust, where workers had tramped and spit uncounted billions of germs . . . meat stored in great piles . . . and thousands of rats would race about on it.

Roosevelt jumped from his chair, screaming, "I'm poisoned!" and threw his breakfast sausages out the window.

It wasn't long before Congress passed the Federal Food and Drugs Act (1906), which authorized inspectors to oversee food-processing plants

World War I-era nurses, U.S. Navy. Opposite: Jonas Salk administers the polio vaccine.

and required truthful labels on food, drink, and medicines. Protecting health, once the task of family, charities, church groups, and the local physician, was now also the job of government.

In the early 20th century, thousands of Americans moved from farms to cities, seeking jobs in new factories. They were joined by a tidal wave of poor European immigrants, crowding into cramped, disease-ridden apartment buildings. Poverty, poor housing, dangerous working conditions, and child labor all led to health problems. When the United States entered World War I in 1917, draft board doctors discovered scores of young men too unhealthy to fight for their country.

America gasped. The United States needed to protect its greatest resource—its people. In 1910 the National Conservation Commission reported:

> Natural resources are of no avail without men and women to develop them, and only a strong and sound citizenship can make a nation permanently great. We cannot too soon enter on the duty of conserving our chief source of strength by the prevention of disease and the prolongation of life.

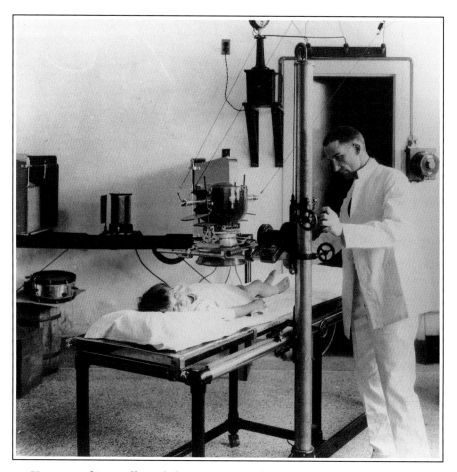

X-ray machines allowed doctors to view bones inside a patient's body.

Better living, better health, a stronger nation. These became goals for the 20th century. Government on all levels tried to improve health care through laws and massive education programs. City and state health boards expanded, followed in 1912 by the formation of the United States Public Health Service.

In 1909 Chicago passed the first city laws requiring milk pasteurization, a process of heating liquid to kill bacteria. At great expense, and after decades of work, cities finished building covered, underground sewer lines that didn't empty into drinking water supplies. In 1914, the federal government set standards for safe water. With water protected and purified, typhoid deaths dropped dramatically.

"AN APPLE A DAY"

For years Americans had depended on foods homegrown and preserved through drying, pickling, and canning. Winter months meant few fresh fruits and vegetables on the plate. But times were changing. City dwellers couldn't grow their own food. So trains, and eventually trucks and airplanes, shipped fresh food from farms to urban grocery stores. Industry moved further into the food business. Large-scale canning boomed in the early 1900s. In 1929 frozen foods appeared in grocery stores.

The first refrigerators, used by industry since the late 1800s, were too large for home use. To keep food from spoiling, most Americans used wooden cupboards called iceboxes. The ice inside kept food chilled but quickly melted and needed frequent replacing. By the 1930s, the invention of small electric motors and nontoxic coolants opened the way for average Americans to own a family-sized refrigerator. With home refrigeration, food stayed fresh longer, with less chance of contamination.

Health also improved with the discovery of vitamins, a group of complex chemicals—found in food—that the body needs to function normally. While scientists did not understand exactly how vitamins worked, they knew a diet lacking certain vitamins kindled illness. Vitamin B deficiencies caused pellagra and fatal pernicious anemia. Too little vitamin C led to scurvy.

An estimated half of American children in 1921 had deformed bones due to rickets, a disease caused by a lack of vitamin D. Health care workers spread the message, and parents responded. Children held their noses and swallowed daily doses of cod-liver oil, rich in vitamins A and D. Sessions in the sun provided the only other protection. During winter months, children donned swimsuits or underwear and "bathed" in the golden light of sunlamps, which—advertisers claimed in the 1930s and 1940s—prevented "colds, rickets . . . worse!"

Food companies began to add vitamins to bread and cereal. Milk fortified with vitamin D virtually eliminated rickets. In 1940, the government published a list of "Recommended Daily Allowances" for vitamins. By that time, Americans were already buying millions of dollars worth of vitamin pills each year as a supplement to their diets.

Though fresher, healthier food was available, many Americans couldn't afford it—especially during the Great Depression of the 1930s. The American Medical Association reported in 1935 that 20 million Americans suffered from malnutrition. To assist the hungry, states established school lunch programs, and in 1939 the government began to supply poor Americans with food stamps, coupons they could exchange for groceries.

Eventually, public health efforts paid off. With vitamins, fresh foods available year-round, and improved sanitation and health care, American children grew stronger and taller with each decade.

HYGIENE (AT LAST)

During the 1920s, public health officials hammered Americans with information about cleanliness. Since saliva could spread tuberculosis, local governments passed anti-spitting laws. Spitting was "becoming a lost art," some health officials happily reported.

Schools promoted daily hand washing, while teachers made "cleanliness attractive" to children. Students starred in plays such as *The Good Health Elves* and *The Trial of Jimmy Germ*. School nurses checked for typhus-carrying lice, watched children for health problems, and dispensed medicine. Life insurance companies encouraged adults to get periodic physical checkups. One 1923 slogan urged, "Have a Health Examination on Your Birthday!"

From nose to toes, Americans cleaned up. In 1931, Kleenex Disposable Tissues advertised: "A new era in handkerchief hygiene! Use once and discard—avoiding self-infection from germ-filled handkerchiefs." By 1937, 80 percent of American homes had hot and cold running water and indoor toilets.

Sunlight substitute

In 1909, the National Dental Association set up the Committee on Oral Hygiene in Our Public Schools. Through the following decades, dentists educated schoolchildren on good toothbrushing habits and the benefits of regular checkups. By the 1950s, dentists were using x rays to detect hidden cavities and were pushing communities to add fluoride, a chemical that prevents tooth decay, to city drinking water.

Even though fluoride proved safe and effective, many people disapproved of its use. Opponents charged that fluoridation of city water was unconstitutional, unnecessary, and dangerous. The 1950s was the Cold War era—a time of fierce distrust between the United States and the Communist Soviet Union. Some Americans feared fluoridation was a Communist plot meant to poison American citizens!

MEDICINE STRIKES BACK!

In June 1900, Dr. Walter Reed arrived in Cuba to investigate yellow fever attacks on American soldiers stationed in Havana. Focusing his attention on the aedes mosquito, Reed proved that the insect transmitted the deadly disease. An all-out battle against mosquitoes began. The military installed sewers, burned undergrowth, and drained standing water where mosquitoes laid their eggs. The results were dramatic. Yellow fever cases dropped from 1,400 a year in Havana in 1900 to only 37 cases in all of Cuba in 1901. Reed's work inspired similar programs in the American South. After more than a century of epidemics that had killed thousands and disrupted commerce, America's last yellow fever outbreak raged in 1905.

But epidemics were not over. One of history's deadliest struck from 1918 to 1919, when 25 million people died worldwide from Spanish influenza. The disease claimed half a million victims in the United States. Frightened people wore face masks, even heads of garlic, to ward off the disease. But influenza spread rapidly when infected people coughed and sneezed. Victims died within days of acute pneumonia. Not until 1943 did scientists develop a vaccine, or inoculation, for influenza.

Many contagious diseases, such as measles, scarlet fever, whooping cough, and rheumatic fever, preyed on children. Quarantining a sick child was almost the only treatment. But, one by one, childhood killers were conquered through vaccination programs. During the 1920s and 1930s, hundreds of nurses vaccinated schoolchildren against diphtheria and traveled door-to-door in hard-hit neighborhoods. Free clinics opened, while newspapers, posters, and radio announcements bombarded anxious parents with the vaccination message.

But medicines and remedies hadn't changed much since the 19th century. Even by the late 1930s, doctors had little to prescribe for illnesses besides bed rest and special diets. Painkillers included opium, morphine, codeine, and heroin. Aspirin, available by 1899, relieved fever, pain, and the inflammation of arthritis and rheumatism. Insulin

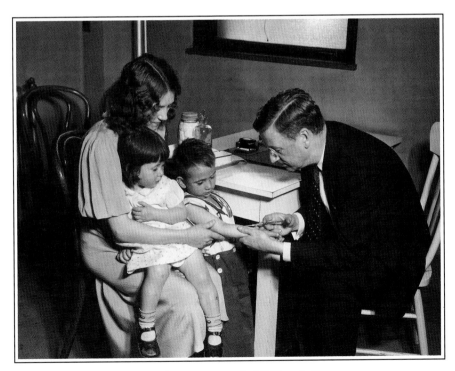

Vaccination prevented childhood diseases.

(available in 1921) helped diabetics, and digitalis gave short-term help for heart disease.

Many other medicines were ineffective or harmful. A 1905 series in *Collier's* magazine noted: "Gullible Americans will spend this year some seventy-five million dollars in the purchase of patent [commercial] medicines." Routinely, Americans in the pursuit of a cure dosed themselves with alcohol, opiates, and narcotics. Many became addicted to the medication.

In 1938, the Food and Drug Administration (a federal agency established in 1931) issued stronger controls on medicine. The FDA cracked down on false claims of wonder cures and required that labels list ingredients and warn that a remedy "might be habit-forming."

The next decade witnessed a medical miracle. In 1928 a British scientist had discovered a bluish green mold that destroyed bacteria—the cause of countless diseases and infections. Through the 1930s, the mold—called penicillin—was produced only in small amounts. By World War II (1939-1945), this lifesaving drug was desperately needed.

In 1941, British researchers arrived in Peoria, Illinois, and began growing penicillin in huge vats of corn liquor. In 1943, American drug companies produced more than 50,000 doses of this infection-fighting medicine. When the government reserved the drug for medical research and sick soldiers, the public was upset. People clamored for the new "wonder drug" to treat their children and families. In March 1945, penicillin finally became available to the public. It effectively treated pneumonia, rheumatic fever, scarlet fever, ear and throat infections, and many other ailments. Millions of lives were saved.

Microscopic organisms called viruses continued to cause disease. One illness caused by a virus is poliomyelitis, better known as polio. Polio attacks the brain and spinal cord, often paralyzing the muscles needed to breathe. Most often, polio leaves victims' legs shriveled and useless. President Franklin Roosevelt lost the use of his legs to polio.

By the early 1950s, the United States was in the midst of a polio epidemic. The disease infected 50,000 people; 3,300 died. Victims lay in

Quarantined sisters, 1953

hospital wards, their bodies encased in "iron lungs"—machines that kept them breathing. Prevention, through vaccination of healthy children, seemed the only answer.

In 1953 came another breakthrough. Dr. Jonas Salk discovered a polio vaccine, and in 1954, the United States vaccinated two million schoolchildren. Polio cases dropped by 80 percent. In 1960, Dr. Albert Sabin developed a longer-lasting polio vaccine, often given as drops on a sugar cube. Thanks to Salk and Sabin's work, polio is virtually gone in the United States.

The American Red Cross collects blood for the armed forces at a donation center in Boston, 1942.

After decades of failed experiments, doctors in the first half of the 20th century learned how to successfully perform blood transfusions—replacing a patient's lost blood with blood of the same type donated by other people. Blood-typing and storing blood for future use saved lives on World War II battlefields and in operating rooms. To make sure blood was always available, the American Red Cross organized "blood banks" and "blood drives," encouraging healthy people to donate about a pint of blood (drawn by syringe). Blood transfusions—joining anesthesia, antiseptics, and antibiotics—paved the way for lengthy, intricate surgeries, including organ transplants.

By the 1950s, the doctor's role was changing. Many Americans had moved away from small towns and city centers to sprawling suburban communities. Doctors no longer made house calls or treated all members of a family through every stage of life. Instead, patients began driving to clinics and large medical offices. Seriously ill patients checked into hospitals.

Doctors couldn't master every area of medicine, so they specialized: pediatricians treated children, dermatologists treated diseases of the skin, cardiologists treated heart disease. One physician noted that such changes brought both benefits and loss:

> If the public could have the advantage of the physician of my father's time—the friend, the counselor who gave that sense of strength to the patients . . . and at the same time be able to have the things that my son [also a doctor] is able to do . . . that would be a lovely thing. But that is completely impractical.

LOOKING TOWARD THE FUTURE

Modern Americans continue to doctor themselves. Drug companies develop thousands of new medicines yearly. Many of these drugs are available "over the counter"—without a doctor's prescription. Store-bought remedies promise relief: antihistamines can clear a stuffy nose; antacids treat upset stomachs.

Americans diet to lose weight, eat natural foods for good health, and shop at supermarkets stocked with fresh fruits, vegetables, and meats year-round. They spend millions of dollars a year on exercise equipment, clothes, shoes, and health club memberships. They monitor their blood pressure, count calories, and buy foods labeled "low fat" and "salt-free."

The hygiene battle has been won—Americans bathe, brush their teeth, arm themselves with household cleaners, and launder their clothes regularly. Soaps, shampoos, toothpastes (with fluoride), and detergents line store shelves. Almost every American house has indoor plumbing, and, weekly, cities haul garbage from homes to landfills.

When the century opened, the average American life span was 47 years. By 1990, a person could reasonably expect to survive to age 75. In 1900, 325 babies died out of every 1,000 born. By 1988, that ratio was 20 per 1,000. Infants and children are routinely vaccinated against a host of childhood illnesses. Americans are healthier than ever. Or are they?

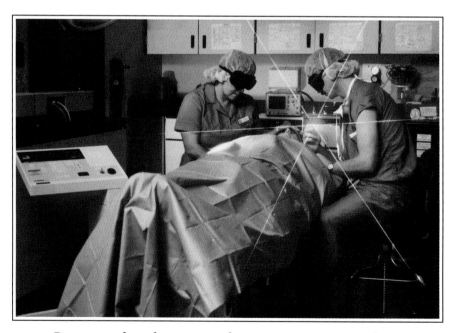

Doctors use laser beams to perform surgery on a patient's eye.

From yesterday's miasma to today's chemical wastes, toxic pesticides, secondhand smoke, and smog, Americans still battle pollution. Contamination of air, water, and farmland has been linked to cancer, a deadly disease marked by abnormal cell growth. Heart disease, linked to smoking, fatty foods, and a sedentary lifestyle, kills more Americans each year than any other illness. In 1981 a new killer appeared in the United States. Acquired Immunodeficiency Syndrome (AIDS) destroys the body's ability to fight disease. AIDS has killed hundreds of thousands of Americans, and many more are infected with the virus that causes AIDS. Can medical science conquer these diseases—diseases that frighten us as smallpox and yellow fever once terrified our ancestors? Are more killers lurking on the horizon?

In their quest for good health, Americans are now looking backward. People are once again turning to soothing herbs and ancient remedies and hiring midwives to help them deliver babies. Even the leech has made a comeback, used for gently draining blood from sensitive areas of the face and head.

More than 100 years ago, Black Elk, a Lakota medicine man, claimed healing shows us "the mystery and power of things." Indeed, even while medical science continues its impressive advance, the cycle of birth, health, and healing, sickness and death, will never lose its mystery or power.

SELECTED BIBLIOGRAPHY

Achterberg, Jeanne. *Woman as Healer.* Boston: Shambhala Publications, Inc., 1990.

Binger, Carl, M.D. *Revolutionary Doctor, Benjamin Rush.* New York: W. W. Norton & Co., 1966.

Blackwell, Elizabeth. *Pioneer Work in Opening the Medical Profession to Women.* 1895. Reprint. New York: Source Book Press, 1970.

Clayman, Charles B., M.D. *The American Medical Association Home Medical Encyclopedia,* 2 vols. New York: Random House, 1989.

Clendening, Logan, M.D., comp. *Source Book of Medical History.* New York: Dover Publications, Inc., 1960.

Duffy, John. *The Sanitarians: A History of American Public Health.* Urbana: University of Illinois Press, 1990.

————. *The Healers: The Rise of the Medical Establishment.* New York: McGraw Hill Book Co., 1976.

Duke, Martin, M.D. *The Development of Medical Techniques and Treatments, From Leeches to Heart Surgery.* Madison, Conn.: International Universities Press, Inc., 1991.

Fatout, Paul, ed. *Letters of a Civil War Surgeon.* West Lafayette, Ind.: Purdue University Research Foundation, 1961.

Jones, Billy M. *Health Seekers in the Southwest, 1817–1900.* Norman: University of Oklahoma Press, 1967.

Kaufman, Martin. *American Medical Education, The Formative Years, 1765–1910.* Westport, Conn.: Greenwood Press, 1976.

Kaufman, Sharon. *The Healer's Tale: Transforming Medicine and Culture.* Madison: University of Wisconsin Press, 1993.

Neihardt, John. *Black Elk Speaks, Being the Life Story of a Holy Man of the Oglala Sioux.* 1932. Reprint. New York: Pocket Books, 1972.

Palmer, Thomas. *The Admirable Secrets of Physick and Chyrurgery.* New Haven: Yale University Press, 1984.

Riley, James. *The Eighteenth-Century Campaign to Avoid Disease.* New York: St. Martin's Press, 1987.

Savitt, Todd L. *Medicine and Slavery.* Urbana: University of Illinois Press, 1978.

Singer, Charles, and Ashworth E. Underwood. *A Short History of Medicine.* New York: Oxford University Press, 1962.

Ulrich, Laurel T. *A Midwife's Tale: The Life of Martha Ballard Based on Her Diary, 1785–1812.* New York: Alfred A. Knopf, 1990.

Vogel, Virgil. *American Indian Medicine.* Norman: University of Oklahoma Press, 1970.

Wilbur, Keith, M.D. *Revolutionary Medicine, 1700–1800.* Old Saybrook, Conn.: The Globe Pequot Press, 1980.

INDEX

Dentist's office, 1905

ACKNOWLEDGMENTS

Photographs and illustrations used with permission of the Bettmann Archive: pp. 2, 38, 43, 44, 46, 50, 53, 61, 66, 68, 75; Corbis-Bettmann: pp. 8, 19, 41, 56, 60, 64, 88; Archive Photos: pp. 6, 13, 21, 71; Manitoba Archives: p. 14; Stock Montage: p. 16; National Library of Medicine: pp. 22, 26, 35, 51, 70, 72; Library of Congress: pp. 28, 31, 84; Georgia Department of Archives and History: p. 49; National Archives, Photo No. 111-B-250: p. 58; Kansas State Historical Society: p. 63; University of Minnesota Archives: p. 77; Tom Merryman, courtesy of Nadine Merryman: p. 79; American Red Cross: p. 80; Brad Nelson: p. 82.

Front cover: Library of Congress